Lau

D0724995

99½
Gross Jokes, Riddles, & Nonsense

Written and illustrated
by Holly Kowitt

SCHOLASTIC INC.
New York Toronto London Auckland Sydney

No part of this publication may be reproduced in whole or in part, or stored in a retrieval system, or transmitted in any form or by any means, electronic, mechanical, photocopying, recording, or otherwise, without written permission of the publisher. For information regarding permission, write to Scholastic Inc., 555 Broadway, New York, NY 10012.

ISBN 0-590-93991-2

Copyright© 1997 by Holly Kowitt.
All rights reserved. Published by Scholastic Inc.

12 11 10 9 8 7 6 5 4 3   7 8 9/9 0 1 2/0

Printed in the U.S.A.   40

First Scholastic printing, January 1997

For Eric Schnurer

Gag Me With A (Fork And) Spoon!

What do you get when you cross crushed ice with a tiger?

A man-eating slushie.

Why did the witch send her pizza back?

They forgot the cockroaches again!

How can you tell a gerbil from a bowl of spaghetti?

A gerbil won't slip off your fork.

What's it called when your mom serves cold, lumpy oatmeal?

Gruel and unusual punishment.

How do you make a maggot stew?

Keep him waiting for a couple of hours.

Why did the customer return his plate with vomit on it?

The cook wanted some feedback.

What's worse than a spoonful of greasy, grimy gopher guts?

Two spoonfuls of greasy, grimy gopher guts.

What's crunchy, brown, and melts in your mouth?

Chocolate-covered cockroaches.

What's red, slimy, and dangerous?

Shark-infested Jell-O.

Wretched Reading

Grooming Nose Hairs by Harry Nostril

Rotten People by Dee Composing

Bad Smells by Ol' Jim Shortz

Noses Run in the Family by Constance Niffler

Flaky Folks by Dan Druff

Furry Disgusting!

Vulture #1: I feel sick!
Vulture #2: What's the matter, did you eat something fresh?

What do you call a pig that wins the lottery?

Filthy rich.

What do you give a seasick hippopotamus?

Lots of space.

What did one snake say to another?

"Let's see you worm your way out of this one."

Do you know that some pigs do their own laundry?

Hogwash!

How can you tell when you're near a chicken farm?

By the fowl smell.

Why do pigs go to discount stores?

Because they're smart sloppers!

What's green and fluffy?

A seasick poodle.

What would you get if you crossed a man-eating tiger?

Eaten.

Did you hear about the pig who ate Cleveland?

He made a hog of himself.

Queasy Does It

What's pink, lumpy, and orbits the sun?

Haley's Vomit.

Bob: Remember that school lunch I couldn't keep down?
Betty: Let's not bring that up again!

What happened to the guy who threw up at work?

They gave him the heave-ho!

Did you hear about the guy who found slime mold in his Oreos?

He tossed his cookies.

Did you hear about the guy whose sandwich fell into a manhole?

He lost his lunch.

Bugging Out

Patient: Doctor, Doctor, I think I'm a house-fly!
Doctor: How long has this been going on?
Patient: Since I was a maggot!

What do you give a 200-pound slime-dripping cockroach with giant teeth?

Anything it wants!

What's a spider's favorite ice cream?

Cootie-frootie.

What do roaches drink at summer camp?

Bug juice.

Why do mosquitos drink blood?

Because soda makes them burp!

How do you make a cockroach float?

Take a big glass of root beer and two scoops of cockroaches!

What's the last thing that goes through a fly's mind before he hits the flyswatter?

His tail.

Chew On This

What happened to the guy who fell into a vat of bubble gum?

He got chewed out!

Did you hear about the girl who sat on chewed bubble gum?

She's stuck up!

What do you call a 300-pound wad of bubble gum?

Chewmongus!

It's About Slime

Why does the Blob make a lousy bus driver?

Because slime waits for no one.

What's the difference between a flyswatter and the Blob?

One shoos flies, one chews flies!

What do you get when a slime monster spits up dinner?

Corn-on-the-Blob.

What does the Blob do all day?

He has a full-slime job!

What happened when the fungus met the slime mold?

It went into culture shock!

Did you hear about the guy who collided with a Jell-O truck?

He had the slime of his life!

Did you hear that the Blob wrote his memoirs?

Well, it's about slime!

How's Your Disgusting Job?

Pig farmer: *"It stinks."*

Garbageman: *"It's picking up."*

Cemetery attendant: *"I have 300 people under me now."*

Plumber: *"It's going down the drain."*

Sword swallower: *"I'm fed up to the hilt."*

Talkin' Trash

What did the dirt say to the rain?
"Thanks to you, my name is mud!"

What's green, has four wheels, and flies?
A garbage truck.

What do you get when you hold a Little League game on a compost heap?

Foul balls.

Why did the mop visit the broom?

It wanted to get the dirt.

What did the rug say to the vacuum cleaner?

"Eat my dust!"

Did You Hear The One About . . . ?

Did you hear the one about the giant with a
nosebleed?

It's all over town.

Did you hear the one about the dirty sock?

It stinks!

Did you hear the one about the quicksand?

It takes a while to sink in.

Did you hear the one about the foot?

It's pretty corny.

Did you hear the one about the fungus?

It grows on you!

Did you hear the one about the cockroach pudding?

Never mind, you'd never swallow it!

Did you hear the one about the slimy ceiling?

It's over your head!

Did you hear the one about the town dump?

It's a lot of garbage!

Did you hear the one about the germ?

Don't spread it around!

Did you hear the one about the mystery meat?

It's a bunch of baloney.

Did you hear the one about the nose?

It never stopped running.

Frightfully Gross

Why did the corpse stay home from school?

He was feeling rotten.

What do you get when ghosts drink soda?

Things that go burp in the night.

What do you call a ghoul who turns eighteen?

All groan.

Losing Your Lunch

What's the difference between a pair of smelly socks and a school lunch?

In an emergency, you can always eat the socks!

How bad is the food at your school?

It's so bad, the roaches phone out for pizza!

How do you make a student fast?

Give him a school lunch!

What did the school cook get you for your birthday?

A gag gift.

What's the difference between a fly and a school lunch?

One's hard to shoo, one's hard to chew!

Have You Ever Seen?

a mosquito bite?

a filthy pigsty?

a sock hop?

a Jell-O mold?

a toilet bowl?

a nose run?

Who Nose?

What did the nose say to the ear?

"Gotta run!"

What kind of train makes people sneeze?

A choo-choo.

Why didn't the nose make the volleyball team?

Nobody picked him!

What did the left eye say to the right eye?

"Between us, something smells!"

Did you hear my nose won the lottery?

Well, you finally picked a winner!

Did you hear about the man who's allergic to his own nose?

That's nothing to sneeze at!

Why are noses sad?

They're always getting picked on!

The Drooling Class

How do young slobs earn extra money?
They baby-spit.

Why is basketball the most disgusting sport?
Because the players dribble.

Have you ever thrown a spitball?
No, and I've never been invited to one.

Monster Mash

Why did the monster spit out the doctor?
It's hard to keep a good man down.

Who won the monsters' beauty contest?
No one.

Monster #1: I don't like your friends.
Monster #2: Just eat your salad, then.

What did one monster say to another?

"What's eating you?"

Why did the Cyclops break up with his girl-friend?

They didn't see eye to eye.

I have three tongues, five arms, green skin, and one eyeball. What am I?

Very ugly.

Nauseating Knock-Knocks

Knock-knock.
Who's there?
Luke.
Luke who?
Luke out—you're about to be slimed!

Knock-knock.
Who's there?
Viper.
Viper who?
Viper nose—it's running!

Knock-knock.
Who's there?
Slime.
Slime who?
'S lima beans for lunch again!

Knock-knock.
Who's there?
Ooze.
Ooze who?
Ooze been telling you all these disgusting
knock-knock jokes?

Giggles 'N' Gags

What do hospital patients tell?

Sick jokes.

Where do smart belly buttons go to school?

The Navel Academy.

What's the first question they get asked?

"Are you an innie or an outie?"

What did the tired shopper say to the guy with smelly socks?

"Your feet are killing me."

What's the difference between a peach and a sore?

One bruises easily, one oozes easily!

Why is someone with a toe fungus like a losing team?

They both know the agony of defeat.

How do you know if someone has false teeth?

It comes out in conversation.

What do you do when a steamroller runs over your brother?

Bring him home and slip him under the door!

What's a volcano?

A mountain with an upset stomach.

What do you call 144 of these really
disgusting jokes?

A gross.

Why do monsters live next to humans?

So they can have them over for dinner.

Knock-knock.
Who's there?
Wooden shoe.
Wooden shoe who?
Wooden shoe like to change
your _underware_ sometime?